DATE DUE

# ACTION SCIENCE

# TREES

**Carolyn Boulton**

**Series consultant: Joyce Pope**

**Franklin Watts**

**London  New York  Toronto  Sydney**

© 1984 Franklin Watts Ltd

First published in Great
Britain in 1984
by Franklin Watts Ltd
12a Golden Square
London W1

First published in the United
States of America by
Franklin Watts Inc.
387 Park Avenue South
New York
N.Y. 10016

Phototypeset by Tradespools
Ltd, Frome, Somerset
Printed in Italy

UK edition:
ISBN 0 86313 132 8
US edition:
ISBN 0-531-04635-4
Library of Congress
Catalog Card Number:
84-50016

**Designed by**
Ben White

**Illustrated by**
Colin Newman, Val Sangster/
Linden Artists,
and Chris Forsey

**ACTION SCIENCE**

# TREES

# Contents

# Equipment

As well as a few everyday items, you will need the following equipment to carry out the activities in this book.

Spiral-bound notebook
Scrapbook
Pencils, including one
  with a soft lead
Plastic bags
String
Pruning shears
Jam jar
Knife
Heavy books
Blotting paper
Thick card
Thin, strong paper

Hand lens on ribbon to
  go around neck
Tape measure
Sandpaper
Crayons
Strong tape
Old white sheet or piece
  of old cloth
Flower pots or yogurt
  pot
Trowel
Soil
Tree field guide

# Introduction

You can find trees almost everywhere you go. They grow wherever there is enough light and moisture. In fact, they grow almost all over the world except in deserts, very cold places and very high mountains. There are thousands of different kinds of trees. All of them are important to the other plants and animals which live around them.

When a tree's leaves fall, they rot and make the soil richer. The roots hold the soil in place and stop it from being washed away by the rain.

A tree's leafy branches provide shade and shelter and sometimes food for many animals. Some tree flowers provide food for insects. And many fruits, nuts and seeds are eaten by people as well as animals.

The wood from trees is also very useful. It is one of our most important materials. We use it for building, for making furniture, musical instruments, boats, matches, papermaking, for making fires and many other things.

Trees beat all the records for living things. The largest living thing on Earth is a Giant Sequoia tree in California. It is about 280 ft (85 m) high and about 80 ft (25 m) round its trunk. The oldest living thing is a Bristlecone pine in America which is nearly 5,000 years old.

# What is a tree?

A tree is a plant like a shrub, a flower or a herb. But it is much stronger, much bigger and it lives longer than any other kind of plant.

A tree can grow to over 18 ft (6 m) high on a single, woody stem. It is a perennial. This means that it does not die down at the end of every summer, as many other plants do. Instead, it lives on from year to year – sometimes even for hundreds of years. Oak trees, for example, can live for between 500 to 800 years and beech trees may live for 250 years. Each year, a tree grows bigger, and becomes taller and thicker.

A tree's one main stem, or trunk, grows straight up from the ground and divides into branches. A shrub is also a woody plant but it is smaller than a tree. It has many stems that spread out sideways from the ground.

Lombardy poplar

hawthorn

◁ Trees grow in all shapes and sizes. The Lombardy poplar is tall and thin and its branches grow upright. It is one of the easiest trees to recognize in the countryside. The hawthorn looks quite different. It is also a tree, but is often cut back and shaped to make a thick, prickly hedge.

Look around you in the town and the countryside and see how different trees can look.

6

## How to identify a tree

There are many kinds of trees. With practice, you should be able to tell one type from another. Look at the shape of the tree and the pattern of the bark on the trunk. Study the shape of the leaves, flowers and fruits. In winter, look at the buds.

Trees are planted to give shelter and to make places look better. Some are grown specially for their wood.

▷ Make a tree map of an area you know well. Draw in buildings, paths and ponds. See how many of the trees you can name.

London plane

cherry

holly

lilac

# How a tree lives

Trees, like other green plants, make their own food. Leaves contain a green substance, called chlorophyll. Chlorophyll changes sunlight into energy. The tree uses this energy to take in a gas, called carbon dioxide, from the air. This mixes with the water drawn from the roots to make food. The food is a kind of sugar. This food-making process is called photosynthesis.

Some of the food goes into making flowers, fruits and seeds; some into the growth of the trunk, the branches and twigs. Some food is stored by the buds which will produce the next year's leaves and flowers. The rest is stored in the roots and twigs to feed the tree in winter when it no longer makes food.

Photosynthesis only happens when there is enough sunlight. The leaves face upward to catch as much sunlight as possible.

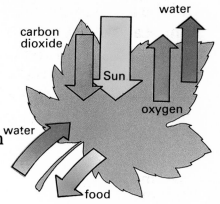

△ Root sap (water and minerals) flows through the stalk and into the network of veins all over the leaf. Sunlight and carbon dioxide ($CO_2$) are needed for making food. Oxygen ($O_2$) and water ($H_2O$) vapor are released in the process.

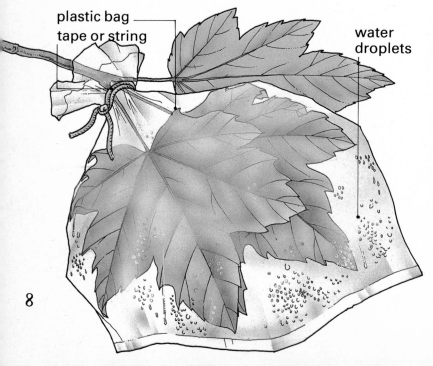

plastic bag
tape or string
water droplets

◁ Water moves through a tree all the time. It is drawn in by the roots and given off as water vapor by the leaves. You can prove this by doing an experiment. On a dry day, tape a plastic bag over some leaves on a tree. If you can find a twig with no leaves on it, tape a bag over it as well. After a few hours, you will see moisture in the bag with the leaves in it. The other bag will be dry.

8

## Air and water

A tree breathes through its leaves. There are tiny openings called stomata on the underside of the leaves. Air enters the leaves through these and oxygen and water vapor are released. As the leaves lose water, they draw up more from the roots through the twigs, branches and the trunk. As well as water, they draw up mineral salts.

▽ Tree roots spread out in a huge network underground. This is often as big as the crown of branches above. The large roots anchor the tree firmly in the ground. The delicate, feeding roots are nearer the surface. These are covered with tiny hairs which draw in water from the soil. Water travels up through the trunk to the leaves.

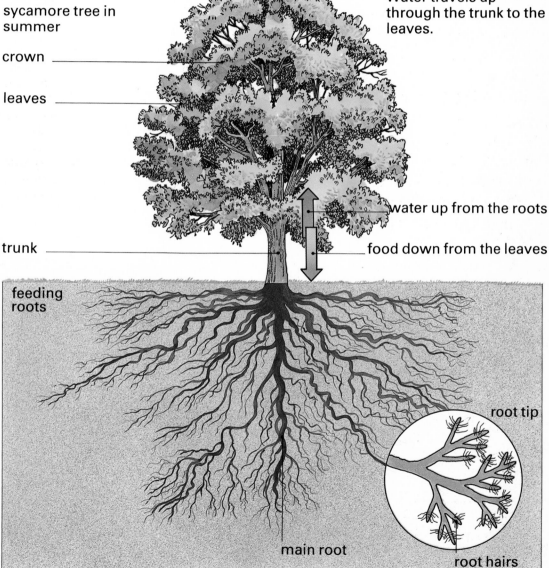

sycamore tree in summer

crown

leaves

trunk

feeding roots

water up from the roots

food down from the leaves

root tip

main root

root hairs

9

# Buds and twigs

▽ The leading bud at the tip of a twig contains next year's main shoot and new leaves. Scales protect the bud. When the bud opens, they fall off, leaving small scars called bud-scale scars. You can tell the age of a twig by counting these. The many buds below the leading bud grow into side shoots. Leaf scars are left when the leaves fall off.

In winter, many trees lose their leaves. But you can still identify them by their buds. Each type of tree has buds with a particular shape, size and arrangement.

Beech buds, for example, are pointed and grow in a zig-zag along the twig. There is only one bud at each joint. Horsechestnut buds are round and sticky and grow in pairs opposite each other. The larch has small, round buds. On some trees, such as the red oak, the buds are grouped together in little clusters.

The buds contain the new shoots, leaves and sometimes flowers. Buds grow in the angle between a leaf and a twig and also at the end of a twig. Many buds are protected with thick scales or covered with furry hairs.

leading bud

bud

leaf scar

one year's growth above bud-scale scars

bud-scale scars

**10**    horsechestnut twig

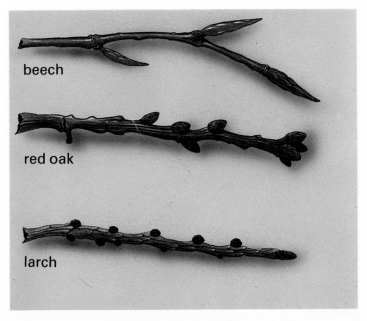

beech

red oak

larch

# The leading bud

The bud at the end of a twig is usually larger than the other buds. It is called the leading bud. It grows more than the other buds and eventually grows into a new branch. As more branches grow and spread out, the "crown" of leaves on the trees grows bigger.

The buds stay closed until spring. In warmer weather, the sap (food and water) flows up to the buds. The tiny leaves and flowers inside the buds swell and push open the protective scales. Then the new leaves expand and unfold.

horsechestnut twig in a jar of water

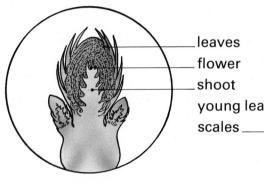

leaves
flower
shoot
young leaves
scales

flowe

△ This is what a bud looks like inside. The tiny leaves and flowers are all folded up.

▷ In very early spring, cut a twig, such as a horsechestnut, from a tree. Do this carefully, using pruning shears. Put the twig in a jar of water on a sunny windowsill. Keep notes of what you see as the buds open and the flowers and leaves unfold. Be patient! The buds may take some weeks to open.

11

# Leaves

Trees are separated into two main groups called broadleaves and conifers.

Most broadleaved trees have broad, flat leaves. They have flowers which produce fruits. The fruits contain seeds. Most broadleaves are deciduous, which means that their leaves change color and fall in autumn. New leaves grow in the following spring.

Conifers usually have narrow needle-shaped or scaly leaves. They are called conifers because they bear their seeds in cones. Most conifers are evergreen. They keep their leaves during winter. They lose a few leaves at a time throughout the year.

wych elm leaf

leaf blade

vein strengthens leaf

stalk attaches leaf to twig

red oak

Norway spruce

12  broadleaved tree        coniferous tree

## Leaf shapes

In summer, you can identify a tree most easily by its leaves. First decide whether the leaves are broadleaved or coniferous.

Conifers which you may see include the Scotch pine, yew, Wellingtonia and larch. The larch is different from other conifers because it is deciduous.

There are many kinds of broadleaves. For example, maple leaves are jagged, willow leaves are long and narrow, beech leaves are oval and holly leaves are spiky.

Some leaves are called simple leaves, because they are made up of one piece. Others have leaves that are made up of lots of leaflets. These are called compound leaves.

▽ Collect some leaves in summer. Arrange them into broadleaved and coniferous groups. Write down all the differences between them.

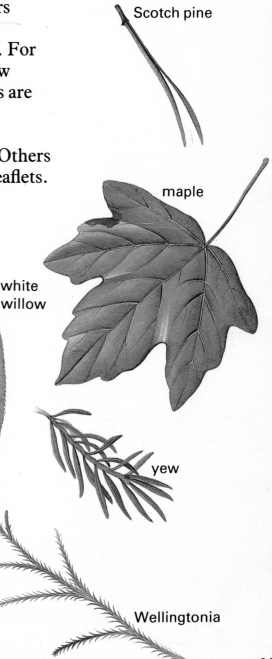

Scotch pine

maple

mountain ash

white willow

ginkgo

yew

beech

holly

Wellingtonia

larch

13

## Deciduous leaves

Leaves are important to a tree because they make its food. In the autumn, as days become shorter, there is no longer enough sunlight for deciduous leaves to make food. It is also difficult for the roots to draw enough water from the cold soil for the leaves to work properly.

The leaves of deciduous trees change color and a corky layer grows across the leaf stalks cutting the leaves off from the twigs. The leaves die and drop from the tree. This helps the tree to survive because it is no longer losing so much water vapor through the leaves.

In spring, when the days start to lengthen, the soil warms up again and the roots can draw up water. New leaves appear.

▽ Making a leaf collection is a good way to learn to identify different trees.
Sandwich newly fallen leaves between two sheets of blotting paper and put heavy books on top to flatten them. Leave them undisturbed for two weeks. Then mount them in a scrapbook and note the name of the tree they came from.

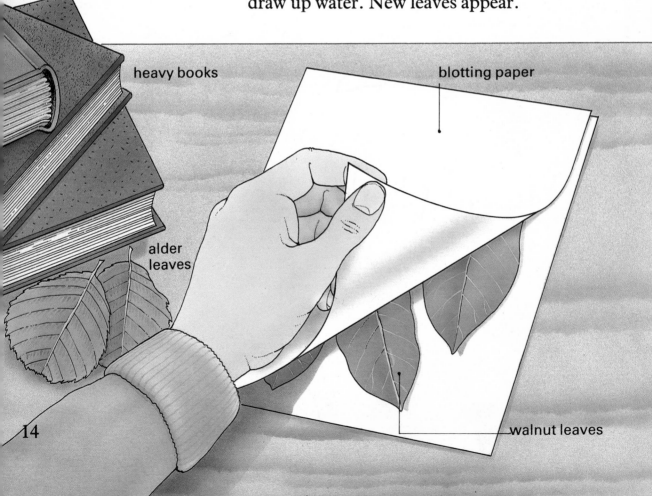

heavy books

blotting paper

alder leaves

walnut leaves

14

## A winter food store

Evergreen leaves can survive the winter for many reasons. They have a thick, tough skin to protect them against wind and often a layer of wax. Both help to slow down water loss. Some evergreen leaves are covered with hairs underneath as well. The bark of many evergreens is very thick and hardy. Many evergreen trees are shaped like triangles, so that snow slides off easily.

Evergreen trees always have leaves and so they can make and store food all year round, except in freezing weather. This means that they grow much faster than broadleaved trees.

Collect some evergreen leaves to compare their feel and looks with broadleaves. Notice too how their veins differ.

▽ You can see the vein patterns on a leaf most clearly by taking a leaf rubbing. Put a leaf upside down on a piece of card. Put a piece of thin, strong paper over the leaf and rub over it evenly with a soft lead pencil. You will soon see an impression of the leaf.

Try doing this with different kinds of leaves. Notice the different vein patterns.

thick card base

thin, strong paper

plane leaf

soft lead pencil

# Flowers

▷ This apple flower is a typical perfect flower. The female parts consist of a long column called the style which leads down to the ovary. The style has a sticky knob on the top called a stigma. This is surrounded by the stamens, the male parts. The stamens contain pollen. When a pollen grain lands on the stigma it begins to grow. It makes a long tube down through the style and into the ovary. There it fuses with an ovule.

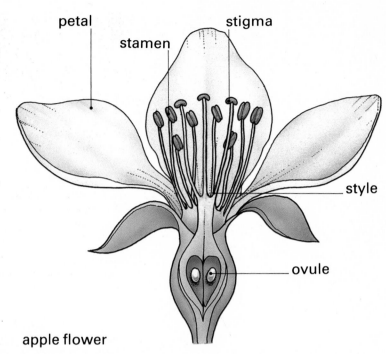

petal    stamen    stigma

style

ovule

apple flower

All trees have flowers, so they can make seeds that can grow into new trees. A typical flower has male parts, called stamens, which produce tiny grains called pollen. It also has a female part, called an ovary, which holds ovules. When pollen from the male stamen reaches the female ovules in the ovary, they fuse. The ovule begins to grow and forms a seed. As the ovule grows, the ovary swells round it to make the fruit.

The process by which pollen is carried from the male to the female parts of a flower is called pollination. This is usually helped either by insects or by the wind. Trees that rely on insects to pollinate them have large, bright scented flowers. These produce sweet nectar to attract bees and butterflies.

△ A bee is attracted by the sweet smell and bright color of an apple flower. Pollen grains stick to the bee. The bee then visits other flowers where the pollen may rub off.

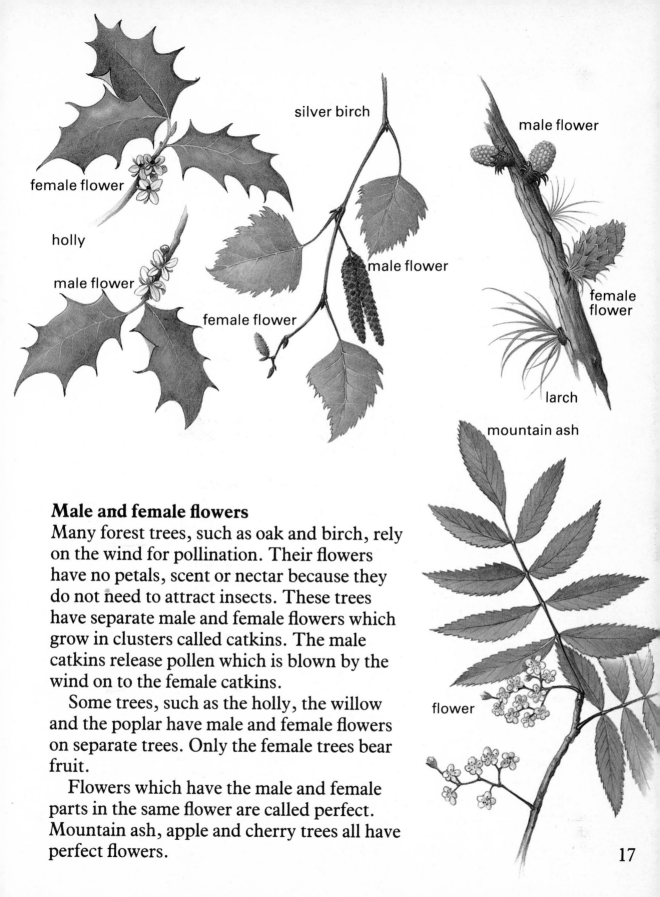

female flower

holly

male flower

silver birch

male flower

female flower

male flower

female
flower

larch

mountain ash

flower

## Male and female flowers

Many forest trees, such as oak and birch, rely on the wind for pollination. Their flowers have no petals, scent or nectar because they do not need to attract insects. These trees have separate male and female flowers which grow in clusters called catkins. The male catkins release pollen which is blown by the wind on to the female catkins.

Some trees, such as the holly, the willow and the poplar have male and female flowers on separate trees. Only the female trees bear fruit.

Flowers which have the male and female parts in the same flower are called perfect. Mountain ash, apple and cherry trees all have perfect flowers.

17

# Fruits and seeds

All trees bear fruits which have one or more seeds inside. The fruits develop from the flowers.

The fruits of broadleaved trees completely surround their seeds. Apples, peaches and pears are all examples of fruits with a fleshy covering. The mountain ash has soft berries. But acorns and walnuts have hard outer shells. Some fruits, such as maple and elm have wings.

The fruits of conifers are quite different and are called cones. When the female cone has been pollinated, the scales of the cone harden and close up. In time, the cone turns brown and the seeds ripen. In warm weather, the cones open and the seeds fall out. Find a closed cone and put it in a warm place. Then you can watch it open.

△ When you eat different kinds of fruit look closely at their seeds. Record how many you find in each fruit and how they are arranged.

▷ Once an apple flower is pollinated, the fruit begins to develop. The ovary forms a protective cover (the core). Inside this, the ovules become seeds (apple pits). The seeds are white at first, but turn brown as the apple ripens.

The stem, just under the flower, swells around the ovary to form the fleshy fruit which we eat. As the fruit grows, the flower parts – the petals, stamens, style and stigma – wither.

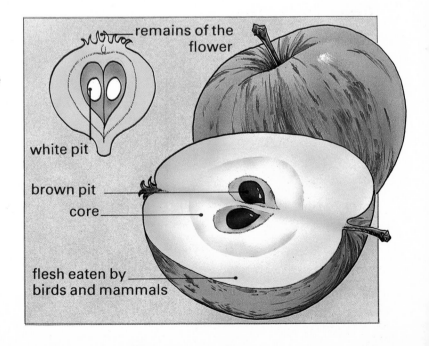

remains of the flower

white pit

brown pit

core

flesh eaten by birds and mammals

▷ Try growing a beech or other tree seed. Soak the seed in warm water overnight. Half fill a pot with moist soil. Put in one seed and cover it with soil. Fix a plastic bag over the pot with string to begin with. This keeps the moisture in. Put the pot in a sunny spot and be patient! In about two months, a seedling should appear. Water the plant regularly.

seed leaves

young shoot

string

plastic bag

beech nut

put stones at the bottom of the pot for drainage

## From seed to tree

The part inside a seed which grows into a young tree is called the embryo. The seed also has a food store. The embryo uses this food store to start growing. First, the seed coat splits and a tiny root grows down into the soil to take up moisture. Two green seed-leaves open out with a bud between them. These seed-leaves provide food for the seedling. They are often not the same shape as the ordinary tree leaves which grow later. In some seeds, the two seed-leaves remain in the seed coat and feed the seedling. Soon, the bud opens. A shoot and the first ordinary leaves appear.

△ Make a note of when you planted the seed and when the leaves appeared.

19

## Animals carry seeds

If a seed falls beneath its parent tree, the young plant will not have enough light to make food and it will not get enough moisture from the soil. So it is important that seeds are carried as far away as possible.

Fleshy fruits, such as holly berries, cherries, apples and plums are tasty food for many animals, particularly birds. But the seeds inside them are inedible. The animal spits them out. Or, they may pass out unharmed in droppings.

Mice, squirrels and birds, such as jays, collect and bury nuts to use as a winter food store. They will probably dig some up and eat them. But the ones that are left may start to grow.

Many seeds do not have tasty, fleshy fruits. Because they do not attract animals, they must be carried away by some other method.

△ A waxwing feeds on the fruits of a mountain ash. The seeds pass out in the bird's droppings far away from the parent tree.

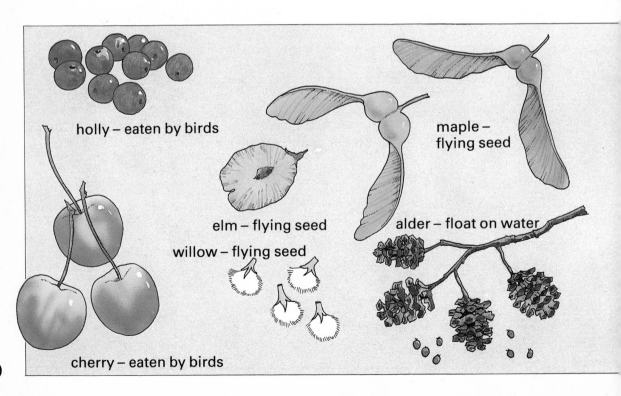

holly – eaten by birds

maple – flying seed

elm – flying seed

alder – float on water

willow – flying seed

cherry – eaten by birds

## Seeds in the wind

Some seeds have wings that act like propellers. The seeds spin and flutter in the wind away from the parent tree.

Some conifer seeds have only one wing. The wing slows them down as they fall. This gives them a chance of being caught up on a wind current and blown away.

Other seeds are very light and have a tuft of hairs which allows them to be blown for miles.

Alder trees often grow by the waterside. Their seeds also have a wing. When the seeds drop into the water they float downstream on their wings. Some are washed up on to the damp riverbank where they may start to grow.

▽ In autumn, collect different tree fruits. Arrange them into groups, according to the way they travel. You can also collect any fruits which have been chewed by animals.

Mark some winged seeds with a bright color. On a windy day, throw them into the air and watch how they travel. Which travels the farthest?

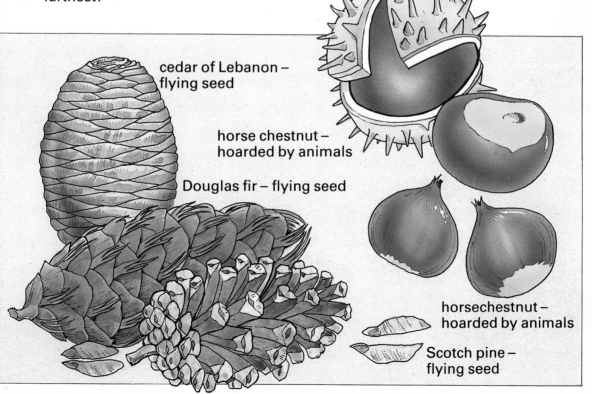

cedar of Lebanon – flying seed

horse chestnut – hoarded by animals

Douglas fir – flying seed

horsechestnut – hoarded by animals

Scotch pine – flying seed

21

# Trunk and bark

Tree trunks are covered with a tough, corky layer of wood called bark. The bark stops the tree from losing water. It also protects it from damage.

Just beneath the bark is a thin layer called bark cambium. This makes new bark each year. Inside this is the phloem layer. The phloem has cells which carry food down from the leaves to the rest of the tree. Moving inward, the next layer is called sapwood. This carries sap (water and minerals) up from the roots to the leaves. Between the phloem and the sapwood is the main cambium layer. New sapwood and phloem grow from this.

The center of the trunk is called the heartwood. This is old, dead sapwood but it is very hard and strong. Heartwood supports the whole tree.

▽ This cut-away drawing shows the different layers of a tree trunk.

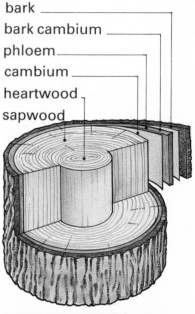

bark
bark cambium
phloem
cambium
heartwood
sapwood

△ The bark of the Scotch pine. As the tree grows older, the bark starts to flake away from the upper trunk and branches. The upper bark becomes quite smooth.

△ The bark of an old sweet chestnut. In a young tree the bark is smooth and pale gray. When it gets older, the bark darkens and becomes deeply grooved.

△ The bark of the beech is a living layer. But on many trees it is dead. It is very thin and delicate and usually stays smooth. It may split up into tiny squares as the tree grows.

cedar

English elm

English elm

△ To make a bark rubbing, use strong, thin paper. Attach the paper to the trunk with strong tape. Rub over the paper firmly and evenly in one direction only with a crayon. Slowly, the bark pattern will appear. If the bark is very rough put some newspaper under the paper so that it does not tear.

Label your bark rubbing with an arrow to show which is the top and bottom.

## Bark patterns

On most trees, the corky bark covering is a dead layer. It cannot grow or stretch as the trunk grows thicker. Instead it splits or cracks into ridges or plates. Each type of tree has a different bark pattern.

Feel the bark of different trees and compare their textures. Notice their different patterns. Never strip bark off a tree. If the bark is damaged in any way, the tree will eventually die. You can keep a record of different tree barks by making rubbings and comparing them. If you can reach a branch, make a rubbing of that too. The branch may have a different pattern to the trunk.

23

# How a tree grows

Every year, a tree grows both upward and outward. The upward growth comes from the leading buds on the twigs. The outward growth of the trunk and branches comes from the cambium layer.

In spring, the tree needs water to allow it to grow. The cambium makes a thick band of wood with wide tubes to carry sap.

In summer, the tree needs more strength to support the weight of all the new shoots. The cambium adds a new band of stronger wood with less space for sap to flow. The two bands together are known as an annual ring because they were both formed in the same year.

▽ You can work out the age of a tree by counting the number of annual rings. Each ring is one year's growth. This is easy to do if you can find a cut tree stump. A conifer forest is a good place to look.

Try to find a recently cut stump. The darker rings are easier to count. You can sandpaper the rings to make them show up better.

△ Use a piece of string to measure the girth of a tree. Hold one end of the string while a friend walks round the tree with the other. Then you can measure the string with a tape measure.

▷ This is one way to work out the height of a tree. First, measure the height of a friend. Ask your friend to stand beside the tree. Stand back from the tree and hold up a pencil at arm's length.

## Annual rings

The size of the annual rings can vary a great deal. In years with plenty of sun and rain, the trunk will grow a great deal and the rings will be wide. But in years when there is very little rain, the rings will be narrow. The rings will also be narrower if a tree suffers from disease or is shaded by nearby trees so that it does not get enough light for growth. Sometimes one side of a tree will grow wider than the other.

The girth, measurement around a tree trunk, can give you some idea of its age. Measure it as high up as you can reach, 4½ ft (1.5 m) is ideal. In many trees, the trunk thickens by 1 in (2.5 cm) every year. If the girth is 96 in (244 cm) the tree is probably about 100 years old. Some species of trees grow much more slowly than others.

how many times higher is the tree than your friend?

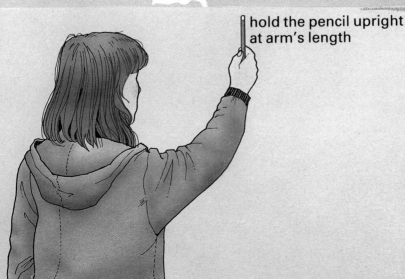

hold the pencil upright at arm's length

◁ Close one eye and line up the top of the pencil with the top of your friend's head. Put your thumb on the pencil at the point in line with your friend's feet. See how many times this part of the pencil goes into the height of the tree.

25

# Changing seasons

Choose a tree you can go to often and study it through the year. Here are some ideas.

**Autumn** Collect fruits from your tree and draw them. Count how many seeds each one has. Record when the first fruits fall. Compare their size with fruits that fall later. Note how far from the tree you find them. Record when the leaves fall and press one.

**Winter** This is the best time to draw the shape of your tree. Notice how the branches divide and in what direction they grow. Take a bark rubbing of the trunk and a branch (if you can reach one easily) and compare them.

**Spring** Record when the buds come into leaf. Look at their arrangement. Note when the tree flowers. Look for nests.

**Summer** Measure the length of shade that your tree makes. Make a note of where nearby plants grow. Look for insects and other animals on the tree.

▷ Keep a scrapbook of your findings with each item dated. First, name and describe your tree. Note whether it stands alone or close to other trees or to a building. Measure its height and girth and how far its branches spread. Compare these measurements in early spring and autumn. Draw sketches or take photographs of your tree each season. See if it changes shape.

winter twig

autumn fruit

autumn

winter

spring flower

bark rubbing

summer leaf

autumn leaf

notebook

spring

summer

27

# What to look for

A tree is the home for many animals and plants. Here are some you might see on and around a beech tree in summer.

The gray squirrel runs up and down the tree trunk. In summer, it may damage the tree by gnawing at the sapwood beneath the bark. In autumn, squirrels eat the beechnuts which fall on the woodland floor. The yellow-bellied sapsucker probes with its thin, curved bill for insects under the bark. Ivy grows up the trunk, reaching towards the sunlight. It uses the tree for support. You may find insects hidden in the ivy.

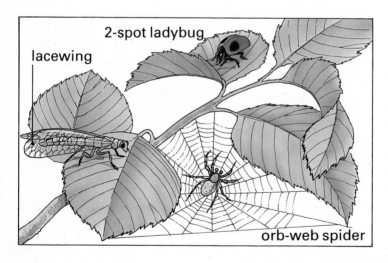

lacewing

2-spot ladybug

orb-web spider

△ Look for small creatures on the beech leaves. You may see the lacewing with its large, flimsy, pale green wings. It feeds on greenfly. The ladybug also eats greenfly. The tiny orb-web spider spins its web across two leaves.

## The beechwood floor

In places where beech trees are growing together, their leaves make a thick canopy. Very little sunlight can get through to the woodland floor, and few green plants can live in such dense shade. Some flowers appear in spring before the beech leaves open. These include violets and columbines.

Fallen beech leaves rot slowly and form a thick blanket on the ground. This provides shelter for many small creatures. The most common are snails, beetles, worms, spiders and field mice. Many birds feed on insects and seeds in the leaf litter.

beating a branch

◁ One way to find out what lives on a tree is to beat a branch. With the help of a friend, hold an old sheet under a branch. Hit the branch sharply with a stick, at a point where it will not break. Creatures living on the branch will fall on to the sheet.

△ Have you ever noticed a thick tangle of twigs on a branch? It is known as witches' broom. It is made either by insects, or fungi or viruses attacking the buds on a branch. The attack causes them to grow in a cluster

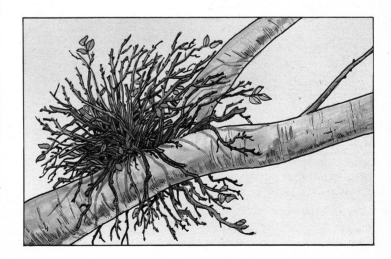

# Glossary

**Broadleaved trees**
Trees that have soft, flat, broad leaves. Most are deciduous.

**Chlorophyll**
The substance which makes leaves green. It traps sunlight to provide the energy needed for photosynthesis.

**Conifer**
A plant that bears its seeds in cones. Most conifers have narrow, needle-shaped leaves.

**Crown**
The part of the tree above the trunk – the branches, twigs and leaves.

**Embryo**
The tiny new plant within a seed.

**Girth**
The distance around the trunk of a tree.

▷ In winter, when most broadleaved trees lose their leaves, you can recognize the different types by their shapes. Holly is one exception. It is an evergreen.
   Coniferous trees also have different shapes, but most of them keep their leaves throughout the year. The larch is an exception.

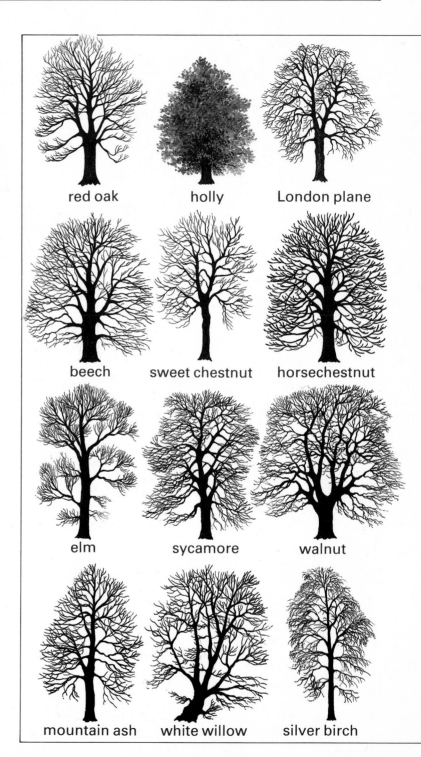

red oak    holly    London plane

beech    sweet chestnut    horsechestnut

elm    sycamore    walnut

mountain ash    white willow    silver birch

30

Norway spruce

Douglas fir

yew

larch

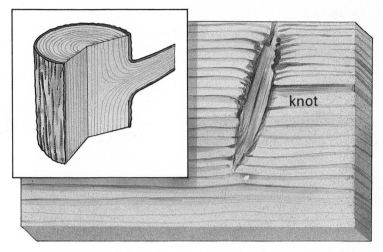

knot

### Lumber
Wooden planks cut from tree trunks. Lumber is used for making a wide range of useful products.

### Mineral salts
Chemical substances which are dissolved in the water a tree draws up from the soil. These substances are essential for growth.

### Nectar
The sugary substance found in many flowers. It attracts insects.

### Photosynthesis
The process by which green plants make food (sugar) from water and carbon dioxide and sunlight.

△ A "knot" is a buried branch in the trunk of a tree. It is the base of a branch that has been grown over by new sapwood.

### Pollination
The process by which pollen is carried, or blown, from the male parts of a flower to the female parts of a flower.

31

# Index